TO THE TEACHER

The THEORY DRILL GAMES are designed to teach Musical Rudiments in an interesting and attractive manner, while saving valuable time at the lesson period. All the work is done at home and the teacher can quickly evaluate the pupils' efforts as the work sheets are handed in for examination.

It has long been recognized that the quickest and best way to master NOTATION, TIME, RHYTHM and all other elements of music, is by means of WRITING EXERCISES. Unfortunately, the theoretical side of music study is usually the least attractive, from the student's viewpoint, and the difficulty has been that of capturing the interest and attention of young pupils to the point where they are willing to do the work by themselves at home.

To help overcome this hazard, the work has been presented here in the form of MUSICAL GAMES or PUZZLES. It offers a DO-IT-YOURSELF plan in that each step is described pictorially in the form of ANIMATED DRAWINGS or COMIC STRIPS, so popular with the average child. This obviates the necessity for lengthy explanations during the lesson period and, at the same time, injects a bit of humor into what otherwise might be considered a "dry" subject.

The Games are presented in LOOSE LEAF form and it is most important that the pupil be given ONE LEAF AT A TIME, not the whole book at once. In this way, the drawings and musical puzzles contained in future games will retain their newness and come as a surprise to the pupil, who then looks forward with anticipation to each successive lesson. For identification, the pupil's name should be written on the front of the folder in the space provided. The set of papers is then kept in the studio and assigned *one game at a time* at the desired intervals.

It will be seen, at a glance, that the THEORY DRILL GAMES are equally adaptable to private or class instruction.

John Thompson

CONTENTS

BOOK TWO

THEORY DRILL GAME, No. 1

New Treble Notes

Pupil's Name_____   Grade (or Star)_____

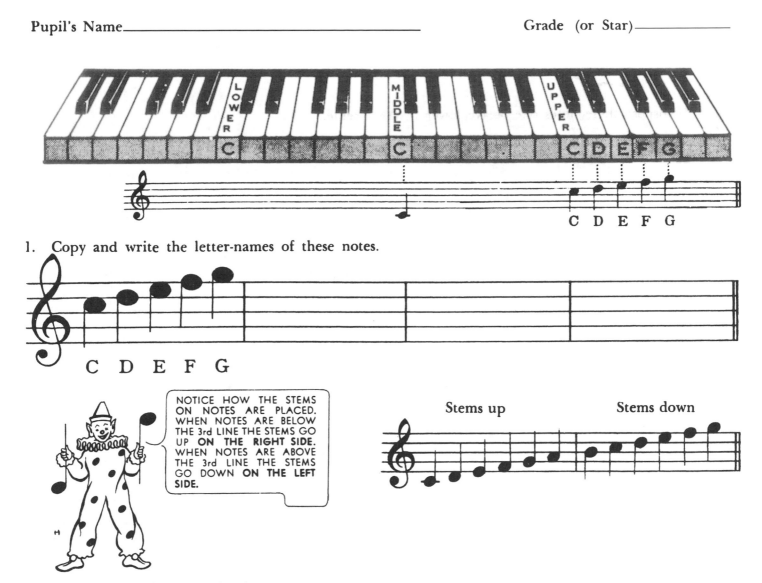

1. Copy and write the letter-names of these notes.

C D E F G

NOTICE HOW THE STEMS ON NOTES ARE PLACED. WHEN NOTES ARE BELOW THE 3rd LINE THE STEMS GO UP **ON THE RIGHT SIDE.** WHEN NOTES ARE ABOVE THE 3rd LINE THE STEMS GO DOWN **ON THE LEFT SIDE.**

Stems up   Stems down

2. Put stems on these note-heads.

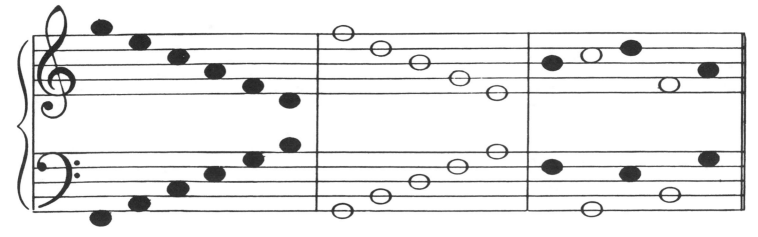

Date_____

YOU NOW KNOW WHERE TO FIND **C D E F G**
IN TWO PLACES IN THE *TREBLE*.
SEE IF YOU CAN TRANSPOSE THEM.
BE CAREFUL OF THE STEMS!

3. Transpose these notes one octave lower in the Treble.

4. Transpose these notes one octave higher.

5. Write the counts in the following.

Counts:

BOOK TWO

THEORY DRILL GAME, No. 2

New Bass Notes

Pupil's Name_____ Grade (or Star)_____

F G A B C

1. Copy and write the letter-names of these notes.

F G A B C

IN THE EXAMPLE BELOW, YOU ARE TO WRITE THE NOTES IN AS MANY DIFFERENT PLACES AS YOU CAN. SOME YOU KNOW IN THREE PLACES AND SOME IN FOUR.

2. Write in 3 places.   Write in 4 places. (2 in each Clef)

| D | E | C | F | G |

Date _____

YOU HAVE LEARNED WHERE TO FIND
FGABC IN TWO PLACES IN THE BASS.
SEE IF YOU CAN TRANSPOSE THEM.
WATCH HOW YOU PLACE THE STEMS!

3. Transpose these notes one octave higher in the Bass.

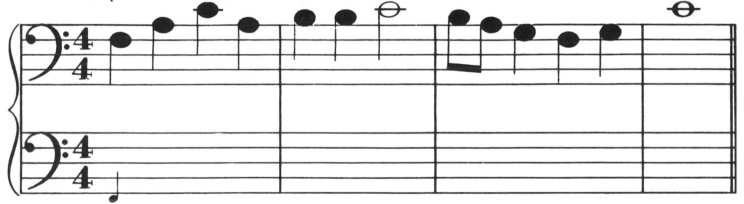

4. Transpose these notes one octave lower.

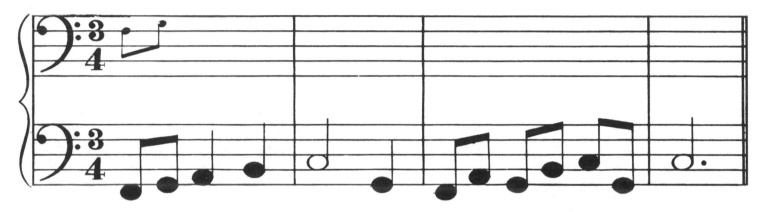

5. Write the counts in the following.

BOOK TWO

THEORY DRILL GAME, No. 3

Black Key Names

Pupil's Name_____ Grade (or Star)_____

1. Make sharps of all these notes, then write their letter-names.

2. Make flats of these notes, then write their letter-names.

Date_____

3. Write the letter-names of the notes to which the sharp, flat or natural signs belong.

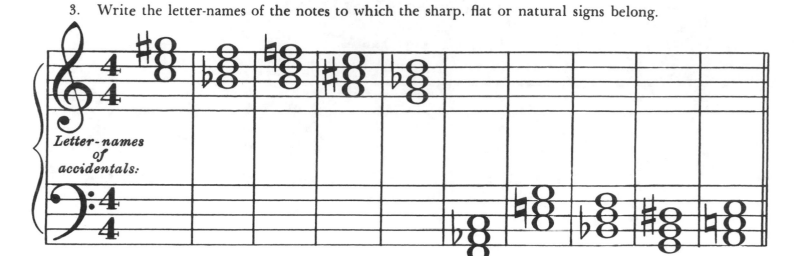

4. Place an accidental before each note indicated below.

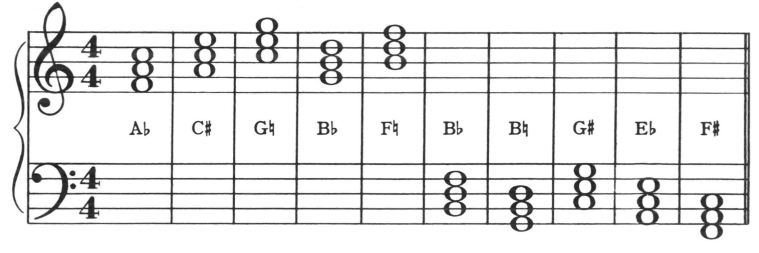

5. Write the letter-names beneath these notes.

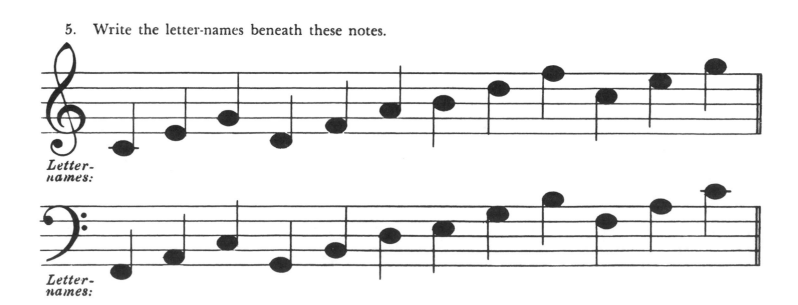

BOOK TWO

THEORY DRILL GAME, No. 4

Pupil's Name _____   Grade (or Star) _____

The Trip to New York

1. Spell the missing words.

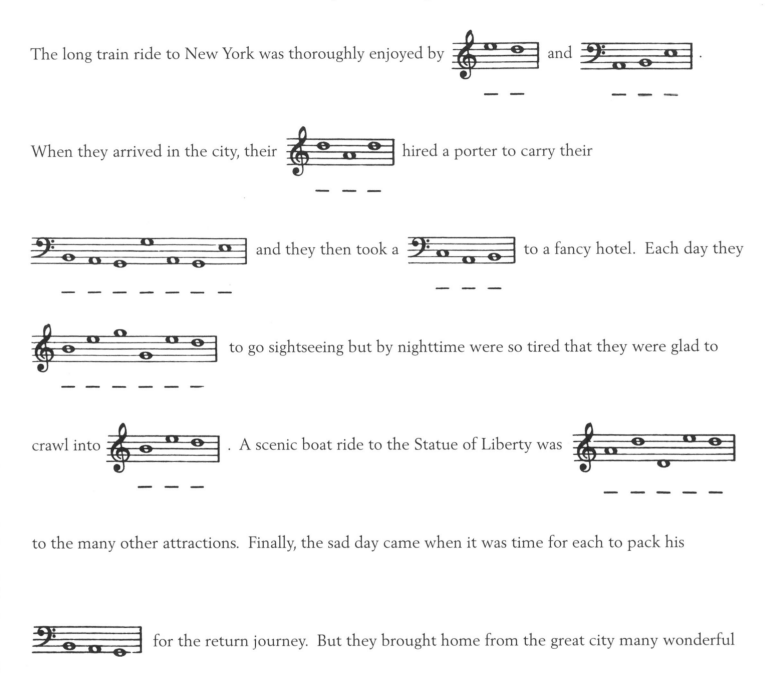

The long train ride to New York was thoroughly enjoyed by 🎼 and 𝄢 .
— —   — — —

When they arrived in the city, their 🎼 hired a porter to carry their
— — —

𝄢 and they then took a 𝄢 to a fancy hotel. Each day they
— — — — —   — — —

🎼 to go sightseeing but by nighttime were so tired that they were glad to
— — — — —

crawl into 🎼 . A scenic boat ride to the Statue of Liberty was 🎼
— — —   — — — — —

to the many other attractions. Finally, the sad day came when it was time for each to pack his

𝄢 for the return journey. But they brought home from the great city many wonderful
— — —

memories that could never be 🎼 .
— — — — — — —

Date _____

8

2. Use *only one Note* to complete these measures — either ♩ or ♪

Counts: 1 2 3   1 2 3   1 2 3   1 2 3   1 2 3   1 2 3

3. Use as many Quarter Notes as needed to complete these measures.

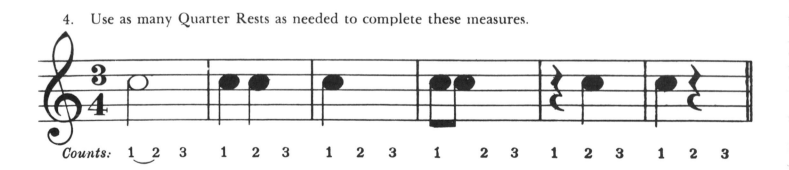

Counts: 1 2 3 4   1 2 3 4   1 2 3 4   1 2 3 4   1 2 3 4

4. Use as many Quarter Rests as needed to complete these measures.

Counts: 1 2 3   1 2 3   1 2 3   1 2 3   1 2 3   1 2 3

5. Here you may use *only one Rest*. It must be either ▬ or ⅄

Counts: 1 2 3 4   1 2 3   4   1 2 3   4   1   2 3 4   1 2   3 4

THEORY DRILL GAME, No. 5

Accents

Pupil's Name_____   Grade (or Star)_____

1. Play the following on your piano and accent as marked. Note that even though the same notes are used in each example, they sound quite different when accented properly.

    a) In Two-Four, accent the first count of every measure. (The accents are marked thus, >)

    b) In Three-Four, accent the first count of every measure.

    c) In Four Four, there are *two* accents. A strong accent on the *first* count and a lighter accent on the *third count.* (Strong accents are marked thus, >   Lighter accents are marked thus, — .)

Date _____

2. Put an accent mark (>) over the first counts in the following.

a)

c) Mark the accents in the following example.

Put this mark (>) over the first count. and this mark (—) over the third count.

BOOK TWO

THEORY DRILL GAME, No. 6

Pupil's Name _____   Grade (or Star) _____

How "Mighty Hunter" Was Named

1. Spell the missing words.

Native Americans usually earned their names from an important 𝄢 ● ● ● _ _ _ _ accomplished

during their youth. One day, an 𝄢 ● ● _ _ _ _ chief sent a young girl out to hunt. It had been

a long, hard winter and food was scarce. In fact, most of the tribe were nearly 𝄢 ● ● ● _ _ _ _ from

starvation. The brave girl put on her 𝄢 ● ● ● ● ● _ _ _ _ _ moccasins, painted her

𝄢 ● ● ● _ _ _ _ and started out with a bow and arrow and 𝄢 ♯● _ _ _ _ _ _ knife.

She 𝄢 ● ● ● ● ● _ _ _ _ _ down near a river and waited patiently for many days, until a

𝄢 ● ● ● 𝄽 _ _ _ _ **R** and a 𝄢 ● ● ● 𝄽 _ _ _ _ **R** finally appeared. The tribe was thrilled and grateful,

and 𝄢 ● ● ● _ _ _ _ on the meat for a long time. For this courageous 𝄢 ● ● ● ● _ _ _ _ ,

"Mighty Hunter" was named.

Date _____

2. Write the counts and mark the accents in the following.

Accents:

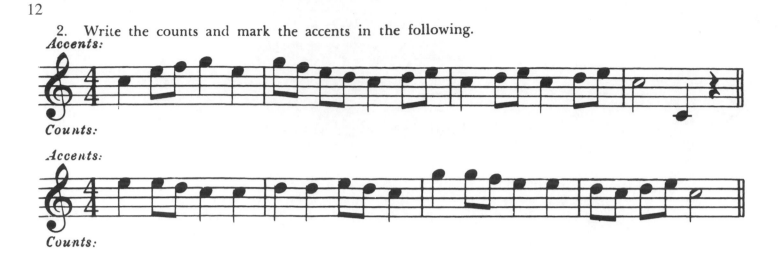

Counts:

3. Add one note to complete these measures. (Either ♩ or ♪)

SPELL THE WORDS BELOW IN
AS MANY DIFFERENT PLACES
AS YOU CAN, USING BOTH TREBLE
AND BASS, AS SHOWN IN THE SAMPLE.

4.

| A D A G E | B E A D E D | D E F A C E D |

BOOK TWO

THEORY DRILL GAME, No. 7

Pupil's Name_____   Grade (or Star)_____

A Quiz Game

1. Write the letter-names and you will find the answers.

a) What is an expert flyer called?

b) On what part of the body are the eyes, nose and mouth?

c) What does a sheriff wear to prove he is an officer of the law?

d) How does a flower look when it is wilted?

e) What is another word for an old proverb?

f) What name is sometimes given to the front of a building?

g) What legal term is used when property is transferred?

h) From what vegetable is cole slaw made?

i) What is another word for erased?

j) What do people check in Railway Stations?

Date_____

14

2. Draw the bar lines through both Bass and Treble staves in the following.

5. There is something wrong with the *last note* of each measure in the following. Correct it by changing the last note into a Quarter Note (♩) , or an Eighth Note (♪)

THEORY DRILL GAME, No. 8

The Tie

Pupil's Name_____   Grade (or Star)_____

The TIE is a little curved line joining two notes on the same line or space — like this:

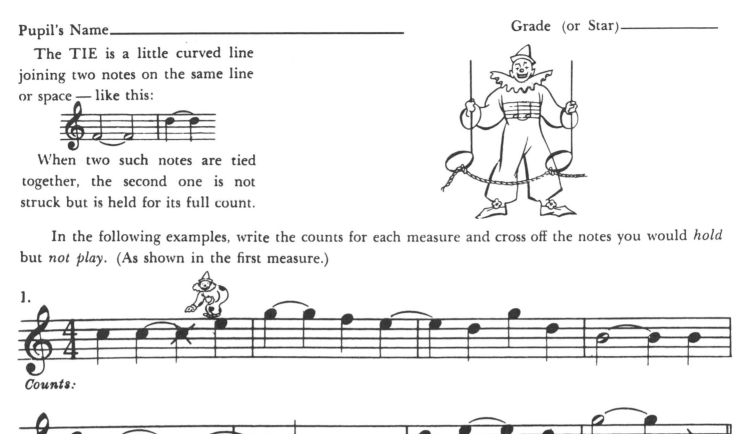

When two such notes are tied together, the second one is not struck but is held for its full count.

In the following examples, write the counts for each measure and cross off the notes you would *hold* but *not play*. (As shown in the first measure.)

1.

Counts:

2.

Counts:

3.

Counts:

Date_____

16

4. See that each measure has the correct number of counts by making Eighth notes where necessary. (Use the beam, thus: 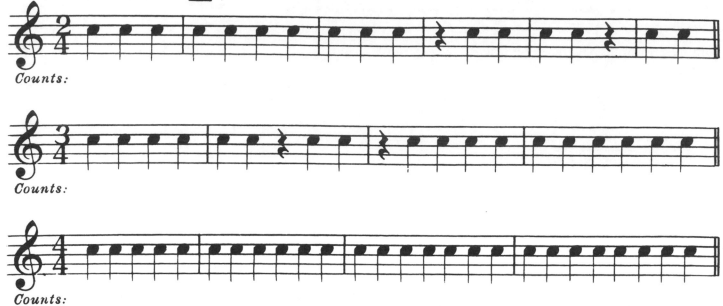)

Counts:

Counts:

Counts:

5. Complete these measures with either notes or rests.

6. Write these notes in as many different places as you can.

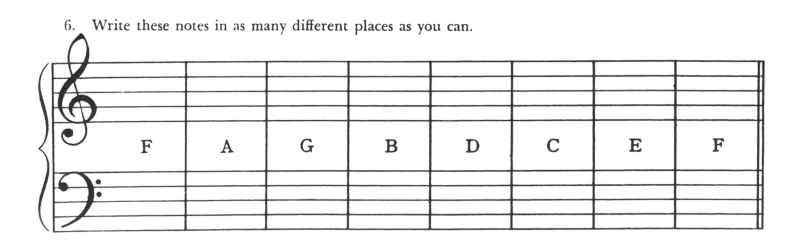

| F | A | G | B | D | C | E | F |

THEORY DRILL GAME, No. 9
The Dotted Quarter Note

Pupil's Name_____   Grade (or Star)_____

Complete the counts in the following by adding an Eighth note or Eighth rest where needed. Watch the counts carefully. Some measures are complete.

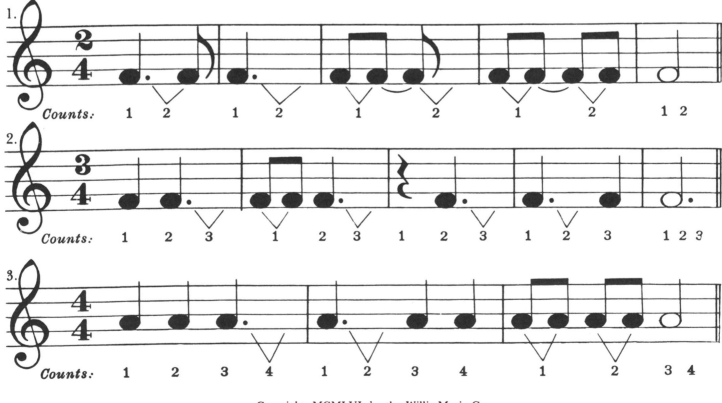

Date_____

Let's see how you are as a **composer** — or **musical arranger.**

Below you will find three well-known tunes. However, the Time Values have not been properly marked. See if you can arrange the notes in correct time so the tunes will sound as they were originally written.

First play the notes on your piano — exactly as they are shown. From this, you will surely be able to recognize the tunes. Then arrange the Time Values accordingly.

Here is a sample to show you how to do it.
Suppose "DIXIE" were written like this.

By making Eighth notes in certain places it immediately takes its proper form.

4. To correct this tune you need only make some dotted Quarters followed by an Eighth note. Be sure you put them in the right places!

5. This piece only requires some Eighth notes and some Ties to make it correct.

6. This tune also needs Eighth notes and Ties. Can you find the proper places for them?

THEORY DRILL GAME, No. 10

Pupil's Name _____   Grade (or Star) _____

The Young Thief

1. Spell the missing words.

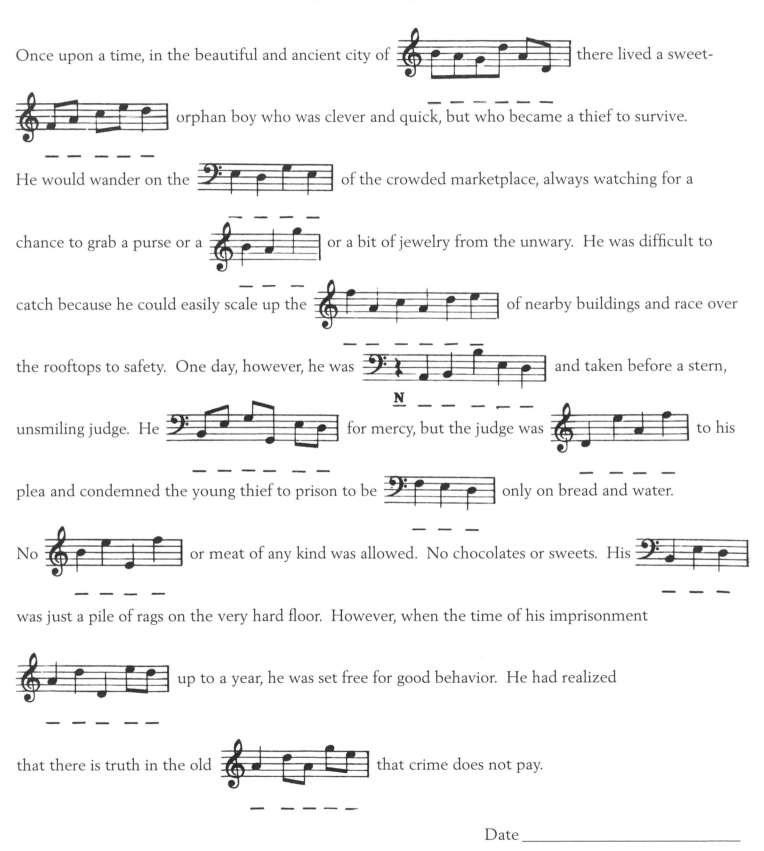

Once upon a time, in the beautiful and ancient city of _____ there lived a sweet-

_____ orphan boy who was clever and quick, but who became a thief to survive.

He would wander on the _____ of the crowded marketplace, always watching for a

chance to grab a purse or a _____ or a bit of jewelry from the unwary. He was difficult to

catch because he could easily scale up the _____ of nearby buildings and race over

the rooftops to safety. One day, however, he was _____ and taken before a stern,

unsmiling judge. He _____ for mercy, but the judge was _____ to his

plea and condemned the young thief to prison to be _____ only on bread and water.

No _____ or meat of any kind was allowed. No chocolates or sweets. His _____

was just a pile of rags on the very hard floor. However, when the time of his imprisonment

_____ up to a year, he was set free for good behavior. He had realized

that there is truth in the old _____ that crime does not pay.

Date _____

A PIECE OF MUSIC DOES NOT ALWAYS BEGIN ON THE FIRST COUNT. BUT, IF THE FIRST MEASURE IS INCOMPLETE, THE LAST MEASURE MUST ALWAYS BALANCE BY HAVING ONLY THE NUMBER OF COUNTS THAT WERE MISSED IN THE FIRST MEASURE. STUDY THE EXAMPLES BELOW CAREFULLY.

2.   First write the counts then the accents in the following. Be careful of the dotted Quarter notes!

THEORY DRILL GAME, No. 11

Pupil's Name———————————————————— Grade (or Star)——————————

1. Mark the counts and accents in the following.

2. The following begin with an incomplete measure.

This begins on the 4th count. Mark the bar lines, counts and accents accordingly.

This begins on the 3rd count. Mark the bar lines, counts and accents.

This begins on the 3rd count. Mark the bar lines, counts and accents.

Date——————————————

THEORY DRILL GAME, No. 12

The Sixteenth Note

Pupil's Name _____ Grade (or Star) _____

1. Make 16th notes of the following. in groups of two by adding stems and double beams.

Make 16th notes in groups of four by adding stems and double beams.

2. Write the counts in the following.

Counts:

Counts:

Counts:

Date _____

3. The 16th Rest looks like an 8th Rest with a double flag.

Trace these 16th Rests, then see if you can draw some of your own.

Mark the counts.

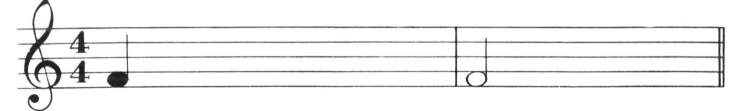

Counts:

4. Complete these measures by adding enough 16th notes. (In groups of four.)

5. An eighth note is equal to . . . . . sixteenth notes.

A quarter note is equal to . . . . . sixteenth notes.

A half note is equal to . . . . . . sixteenth notes

A whole note is equal to . . . . . sixteenth notes.

A dotted half note is equal to . . . . sixteenth notes.

A dotted quarter note is equal to . . . sixteenth notes.

PUT ON YOUR THINKING CAP AND SEE HOW MANY OF THE ABOVE QUESTIONS YOU CAN ANSWER CORRECTLY.

THEORY DRILL GAME, No. 9

Six-Eight Time

Pupil's Name——————————————————————— Grade (or Star)———————

1. First write the counts for the following, then mark the accents. using ꝰ for the strong accent and ꝑ for the lighter accent.

2. In the following, make 8th notes in groups of three (using stems and a beam). Next, draw in the bar lines and mark the counts and accents.

Date———————————

26

TIME VALUES IN SIX-EIGHT
An eighth note gets one full count.
A quarter note gets two full counts.
A dotted quarter gets three full counts.
There are two 16ths to one full count.

3. Mark the counts and accents.

Accents:

Counts:

4. Complete these measures, using either 8th notes or 8th rests.

5. Draw bar lines in the following — then mark the counts and accents.

Accents:

Counts:

Accents:

Counts:

BOOK TWO

THEORY DRILL GAME, No. 14

The Triplet

Pupil's Name_____   Grade (or Star)_____

1. Mark the counts in the following.

Counts:

Counts:

Counts:

2. Make Triplets of the following by using stems, a beam, the curved line ⌒ and the figure ３

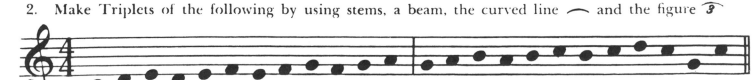

Date_____

28

THEORY DRILL GAME, No. 15

Pupil's Name_____   Grade (or Star)_____

1. Spell these words in both Clefs in quarter notes. ♩

D E F A C E D	B A G G A G E	C A B B A G E

2. Spell in both Clefs. Score them as 8th notes in pairs. ♫ ♫

E D G E	C A G E	F A D E	B E A D

3. Spell in both Clefs. Write as triplets, two to each measure. ♫³ ♫³

F A C A D E	B E G G E D	D E E D E D

4. Spell the words in 16ths — both Clefs. ♬

C A F E	G A G E	D E A F	F A C E

Date_____

5. Help the little clown pass this final test.

Write the answers for him in his balloon.

Having successfully completed this book, the pupil should be assigned **THEORY DRILL GAMES, BOOK THREE.**